Disappearing Forests

Angela Royston

Heinemann
LIBRARY

www.heinemann.co.uk/library
Visit our website to find out more information about Heinemann Library books.

To order:
☎ Phone 44 (0) 1865 888066
🖹 Send a fax to 44 (0) 1865 314091
💻 Visit the Heinemann Bookshop at www.heinemann.co.uk/library to browse our catalogue and order online.

First published in Great Britain by Heinemann Library, Halley Court, Jordan Hill, Oxford OX2 8EJ, part of Harcourt Education. Heinemann is a registered trademark of Harcourt Education Ltd.

Editorial: Sian Smith and Cassie Mayer
Design: Joanna Hinton-Malivoire
Picture research: Melissa Allison, Fiona Orbell and Erica Martin
Production: Duncan Gilbert
Printed and bound in China by South China Printing Co. Ltd.

ISBN 978 0 431 08477 0
12 11 10 09 08
10 9 8 7 6 5 4 3 2 1

British Library Cataloguing in Publication Data
Royston, Angela
   Disappearing forests. - (Protect our planet)
   1. Deforestation - Juvenile literature 2. Deforestation
   - Control - Juvenile literature
   I. Title
   333.7'5

Acknowledgements
The publishers would like to thank the following for permission to reproduce photographs: © Alamy p.**25** (Asia); © Corbis pp.**11**, **23** (Craig Tuttle), **12** (Joel W. Rogers); © Ecoscene pp.**15** (Erik Schaffer), **24** (Simon Grove), **14** (Wayne Lawler); © Getty Images pp.**29** (AFP), **7** (Eric Jacobson), **28** (Johner Images), **20**, **9** (Photodisc); © Nature Picture Library pp.**17** (Luiz Claudio Marigo), **10** (Staffan Widstrand); © Panos pp.**19** (Dean Sewell), **22** (Georg Gerster), **26** (Gerd Ludwig), **18** (Paul Lowe), **16** (Rob Huibers), **13** (Sven Torfinn); © Pearson Education Ltd. **27** (Tudor Photography); © Photolibrary pp.**6** (Alex L Fradkin), **5** (Jon Arnold Images), **21** (Richard Packwood)

Cover photograph of forest debris reproduced with permission of © Corbis (Joel W. Rogers).

Every effort has been made to contact copyright holders of any material reproduced in this book. Any omissions will be rectified in subsequent printings if notice is given to the publishers.

Contents

Any words appearing in the text in bold, **like this**, are explained in the Glossary.

What are forests?

Forests are large areas where many trees grow. Tropical forests are the biggest forests. They grow near the **Equator**. Huge forests of fir trees grow in cold countries near the **Arctic**.

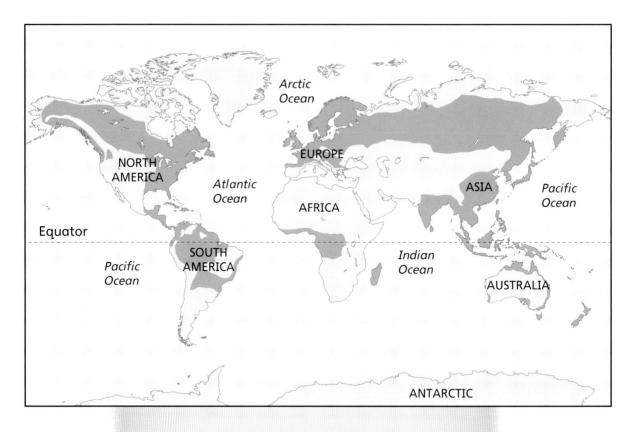

Forests are shown in green on this map of the world.

This tropical forest is in Costa Rica.

Some forests have many different kinds of trees and plants. Other forests have mostly one kind of tree. Both kinds of forest are in danger. Many of their trees are being destroyed.

Why are forests important?

Forests are important for several reasons. Many different kinds of plants and animals live in them. Most of these plants and animals cannot live in other places. Only the forest gives them the food and shelter they need.

The bark, leaves, and plants in the forest give this elk all the food it needs.

The rain and heat in the rainforests mean that flowers and fruit grow all year round.

Rainforests are especially important. More different kinds of plants and animals live here than anywhere else. Scientists are still finding new kinds of rainforest insects, animals, and plants.

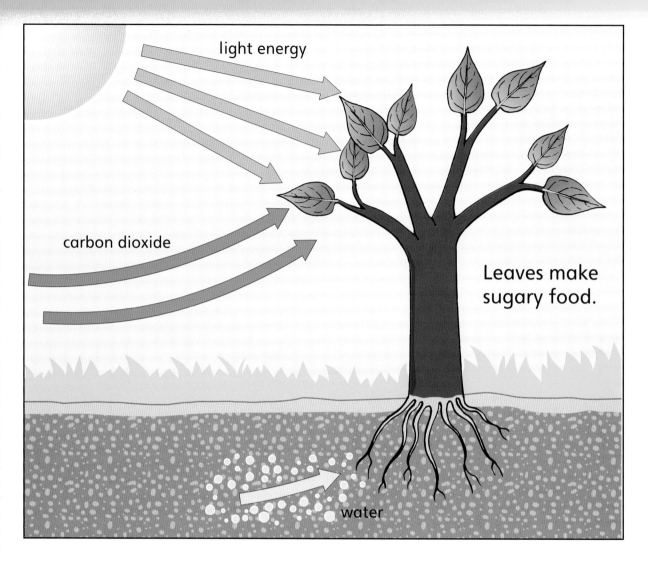

light energy

carbon dioxide

Leaves make
sugary food.

water

Forests help to keep the air fresh and
healthy for living things to breathe. Green
leaves take in the gas **carbon dioxide** from
the air. They use sunlight to change carbon
dioxide and water into plant food.

When leaves make plant food, they also make **oxygen**. The oxygen mixes with the air. Most land animals need to breathe in oxygen from the air to stay alive.

How people use forests

People who live in a rainforest find all the food and shelter they need there. Much of the food that we now eat first came from the rainforest. Long ago, people took plants and animals from the rainforest and started farming them in other places.

All of these foods were first found in rainforests.

This paper mill makes paper from the wood of fir trees.

Fir trees grow well near the **Arctic**. They are cut down and their wood is used to make furniture, doors, and other things. Most paper is made from trees that grow here.

11

Cutting down rainforests

Half the trees on this hillside
have been cut down.

People are cutting down millions of trees
in rainforests. These people work for
companies that are clearing the land for
farming. Some companies sell the wood to
people in other countries.

Sometimes these companies use huge bulldozers to cut down many trees at once. Sometimes they clear the forest by burning the trees. Many rainforests are becoming much smaller.

This bulldozer has cut down many trees to make a road through the rainforest.

What happens when trees are gone?

The **roots** of trees help to hold soil in place. When it rains, the roots of the trees suck up large amounts of water.

roots

Soil has been washed away, leaving deep lines in the ground.

When the trees are cut down, the rain washes the soil away. This is called **erosion**. All the water runs into rivers and can cause floods.

Making farmland

People clear parts of the rainforest to grow farm **crops**. Farmers grow just one kind of plant, such as oil palms or rubber trees. All the different kinds of plants that grew there before are destroyed.

This land used to be covered with many different plants and trees. Now it is used to grow oil palm plants.

These cattle in Brazil are being fed on land that used to be rainforest.

Some farmers plant grass for large herds of cattle to eat. The soil is so thin, the grass only grows for a few years. When the grass can no longer grow there, the farmers cut down more trees to plant new grass.

Forest fires

Fires are destroying large areas of forests. Some fires are started on purpose by farmers to clear the land. The smoke from big fires **pollutes** the air for hundreds of miles.

Smoke makes the air unhealthy to breathe.

Large forest fires are difficult to put out.

Other fires begin by accident. In summer some forests become dry. This makes fire spread quickly. Sometimes houses on the edge of towns and cities burn down.

Acid rain

Forests are also being damaged by **pollution** from factories and **power stations**. Smoke and gases from factories and power stations escape into the air. The smoke and gases mix into the rain. This is called **acid rain.**

Acid rain kills the leaves of trees. Once the leaves are damaged, the trees die. Some forests are losing many trees because of acid rain.

Most of the trees in this forest have been killed by acid rain.

Saving forests

Forests used to cover much of the land. Today many forests have been cut down or damaged. Most scientists agree that we must save the forests that remain. By saving the forests, we can save the plants and animals that live there.

Hundreds of years ago forests covered all this land.

This forest in Washington in the United States has been protected. It has been made into a national park.

Some **organizations** try to get people to help save forests. For example, the Rainforest Foundation helps people who live in rainforests to protect the forests and the way they live.

Saving rainforest wood

Some rainforest trees, such as mahogany and teak, have very hard wood. The wood lasts a long time and so it is valuable.

Rainforest trees are hard to replace. A mahogany tree takes more than 100 years to grow this tall.

These statues have been made from rainforest wood.

When these trees are cut down, the wood is sold. People in other countries buy it to make window frames, floors, and furniture. If people stop buying things made of wood from rainforests trees, then fewer trees will be cut down.

Replacing forests

Fir trees grow much faster than rainforest trees. Young fir trees only take a few years to grow big enough to replace trees that have been cut down.

Check the things you buy that are made from trees. See if they come from sustainable forests.

Some companies always plant new trees to replace fir trees they have cut down. These forests are called **sustainable forests**. People can help to save forests by buying paper and wood from sustainable forests.

Saving paper

If people use less paper, fewer trees need to be cut down. One way of saving paper is to reuse old paper, such as wrapping paper.

Recycling one tonne of paper saves 17 trees from being cut down.

Recycling paper also means that fewer trees are cut down. Newspapers, magazines, and cardboard are processed and made into more paper. We can all help to protect the forests by recycling.

Glossary

acid rain rain that kills leaves and eats away at buildings

Arctic frozen sea and land around the North Pole

carbon dioxide one of the gases in the air

crop plants grown by farmers to sell or use

Equator imaginary line around the centre of the Earth

erosion when soil or parts of the ground are washed away

organization group of people who work together to achieve something

oxygen one of the gases in the air

pollute make dirty

pollution dirt or waste gases or chemicals

power station building where electricity is made

recycling processing used materials so that they can be used again

roots part of a plant that grows in the soil. Roots take in water and anchor the plant in the soil.

sustainable forest forest in which new trees are planted to replace trees that have been cut down

Find out more

Books to read

My World of Geography: Forests, Angela Royston
(Heinemann Library, 2006)

*Reading Power: Man-made Disasters, Fading Forests: The
Destruction of our Rainforests*, August Greeley (PowerKids
Press, 2003)

Reduce, Reuse, Recycle: Paper, Alexandra Fix
(Heinemann Library, 2007)

Websites to visit

www.greenpeace.org/international/campaigns/forests/kff
A website with lots of information about what children are doing
to save forests. It also gives you information about ancient forests
and what you can do to help.

www.rainforestfoundationuk.org/s-Kids
This website tells you about the people, plants and animals that
live in rainforests. It also tells you about threats to the rainforest
and what you can do to help.

www.srl.caltech.edu/personnel/krubal/rainforest/serve–home.html
Packed with facts, quizes, and lots of information this website tells you
about rainforests. It looks at the plants, animals, and people who live
there, and how we can help to protect them.

Index